Life Love &
Laughter

Aliya Alam

Presentation by *BookLeaf Publishing*

Web: www.bookleafpub.com

E-mail: info@bookleafpub.com

ISBN: 9789357210102

First edition 2022

DEDICATION

To my family…..

Forever Broken?

As gentle as a heart
With a passion so sweet
Here comes the heart who had to retreat
As it broke it grew forgotten
To the broken heart
Who lived unwanted

Two Faces

Outside I am smiling
Almost as tears of joy
But I am sad
Like a broken toy
As a puzzle piece missing
I feel a miss
A snow storm inside me a blizzard
A stormy mist

Weakened

3

Never weaken your limits
Times flies, people change
Hearts grow
But never listen to the haters

Horizon

Without being happy
Nothing would be true
Love would be fake
Trust would fly sorrow

Flaws

5

True love
Is when they appreciate the flaws
Try to realize inside
That nobody is perfect

Heart & Soul

If you try
You can achieve
Put your heart into it
It will happen
But if you love
Even dreams can come true

Rainbows

7

No matter what happens
Even sadness
Could form a rainbow

Limits

I am happy
I learned how to smile
I try to be what others expect
But you will never fulfill those expectations
You have to achieve your own

Wedding Chime

When weddings happens
Parents will cry
Bridesmaid will make the flowers fly
The groom will wear a suit and tie
People will come for fancy feast
Foods for all to eat
Cake is there for a sweet treat
Indoor or outdoor there is no fuss
Getting married is no rush

Tried

I'm trying
Is it good enough
Only if you think so
I will never be what I expect
I feel the pressure
To be great
I am great

I Remember

I remember
Trying to improve myself
Saying that I will never be like anybody else
The only thing I remember is
Wondering inside
Can I do it?

Rare Times

Why do good times
Have to be so rare
Why is it that we can't find trust
In the times we share
Why is it rare to find a smile on my face
These rare times

Mind Games

13

So many things
Inside my mind
Can I break free
I hear a voice in the distance
A good heart makes change
And a good person inspires others

Can I

People ask me
Do you smile
Can you be happy
Can you try harder
I simply say
Only if I want

Expectations by Generations

15

Why do you expect so much
When I fail
All you see is what's on paper
Can't you see how hard I try
Achieving isn't an easy task

Bee Me

A bee
Working hard every day
Appreciated, never
So much to offer
Overflowing with potential
Used but never seen

Wonderland

17

Appreciation is required
Done but never seen
Trust and faith
But shattered so easily
Like broken glass

For Me

I've waited every day
For a moment so great
Where I will be appreciated
celebrated
Free to be me
Only me